INVENTIONS AND DISCOVERY

MARIE ✳ CURIE
AND
RADIOACTIVITY

by Connie Colwell Miller

illustrated by Scott Larson and
Mark Heike

Consultant:
Spencer Weart, Director
Center for History of Physics
American Institute of Physics
College Park, Maryland

Capstone
press

Mankato, Minnesota

Graphic Library is published by Capstone Press,
151 Good Counsel Drive, P.O. Box 669, Mankato, Minnesota 56002.
www.capstonepress.com

Printed in the United States of America

1 2 3 4 5 6 11 10 09 08 07 06

Library of Congress Cataloging-in-Publication Data
Miller, Connie Colwell, 1976–
Marie Curie and radioactivity / by Connie Colwell Miller; illustrated by Scott Larson and Mark Heike.
p. cm.—(Graphic library. Inventions and discovery)
Summary: "In graphic novel format, tells the story of Marie Curie's discovery of radium and radioactivity"—Provided by publisher.
Includes bibliographical references and index.
ISBN-13: 978-0-7368-6486-2 (hardcover)
ISBN-10: 0-7368-6486-5 (hardcover)
ISBN-13: 978-0-7368-7521-9 (softcover pbk.)
ISBN-10: 0-7368-7521-2 (softcover pbk.)
1. Curie, Marie, 1867–1934—Juvenile literature. 2. Chemists—Poland—Biography—Juvenile literature. 3. Radioactivity—Juvenile literature. 4. Radium—Juvenile literature. I. Larson, Scott, 1959– ill. II. Heike, Mark, ill. III. Title. IV. Series.
QD22.C8M55 2007
540.92—dc22 2006007140

Designers
Alison Thiele and Ted Williams

Editor
Christopher Harbo

Editor's note: Direct quotations from primary sources are indicated by a yellow background.

Direct quotations appear on the following pages:

Page 17, from Marie Curie's letter to Joseph Sklodèovski, December 11, 1903, as printed in Eve Curie's *Madame Curie: A Biography* (Garden City, N.Y.: Doubleday, Doran and Company, Inc., 1938).

Page 18, from Pierre Curie's letter to George Gouy, November 7, 1905, as printed in Eve Curie's *Madame Curie: A Biography* (Garden City, N.Y.: Doubleday, Doran and Company, Inc., 1938).

Page 22, from Marie Curie's letter to Bronya Dluska, November 10, 1920, as printed in Eve Curie's *Madame Curie: A Biography* (Garden City, N.Y.: Doubleday, Doran and Company, Inc., 1938).

TABLE OF CONTENTS

CHAPTER 1
THE CURIES

In 1897, Marie Curie and her husband Pierre lived in Paris, France. Marie had moved to Paris from Poland in 1891 to study physics and math at a university called the Sorbonne. At the time, the Sorbonne was the only school in Europe that allowed women to attend. Pierre ran the laboratory at the Municipal School of Industrial Physics and Chemistry.

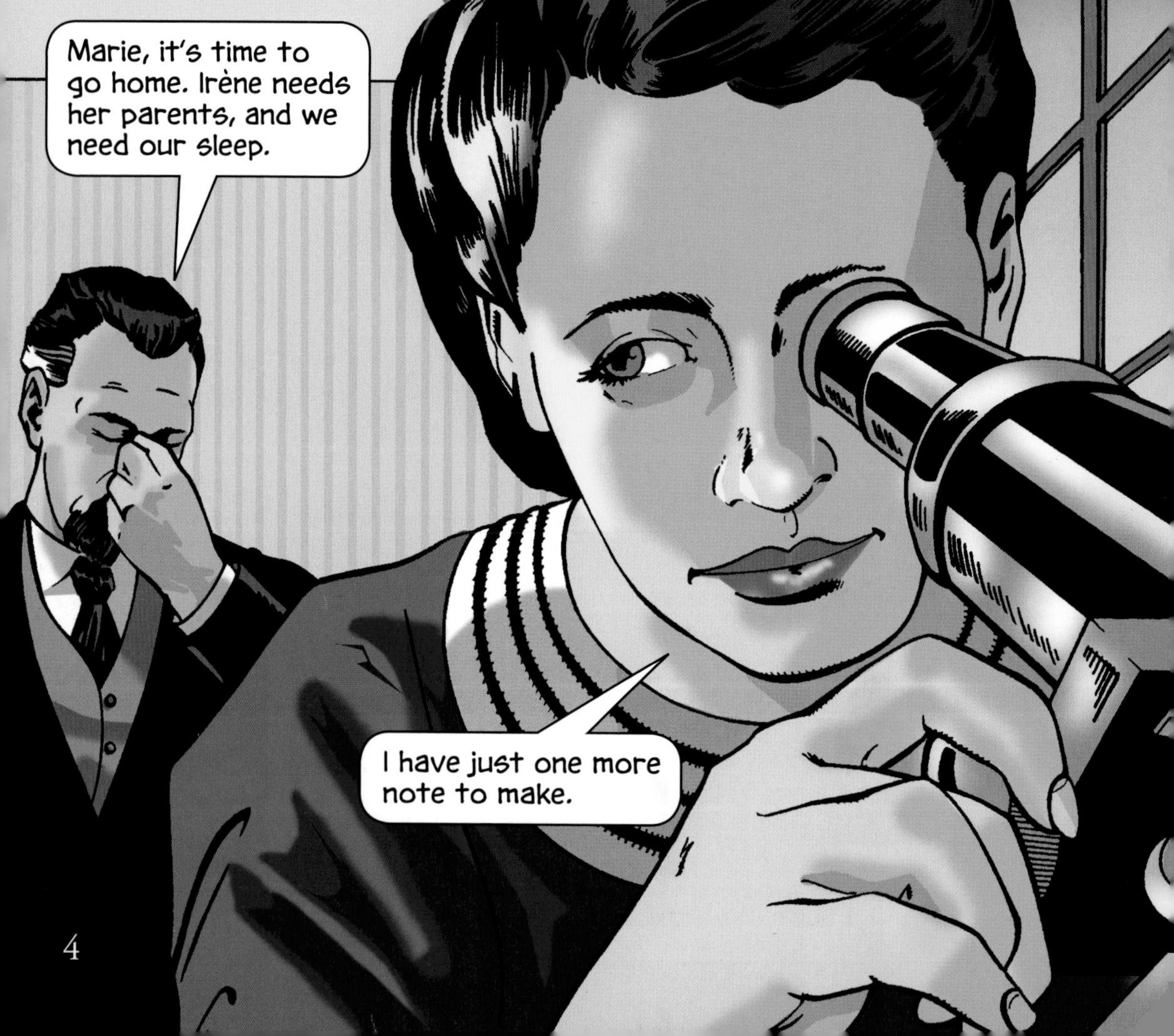
Marie, it's time to go home. Irène needs her parents, and we need our sleep.
I have just one more note to make.

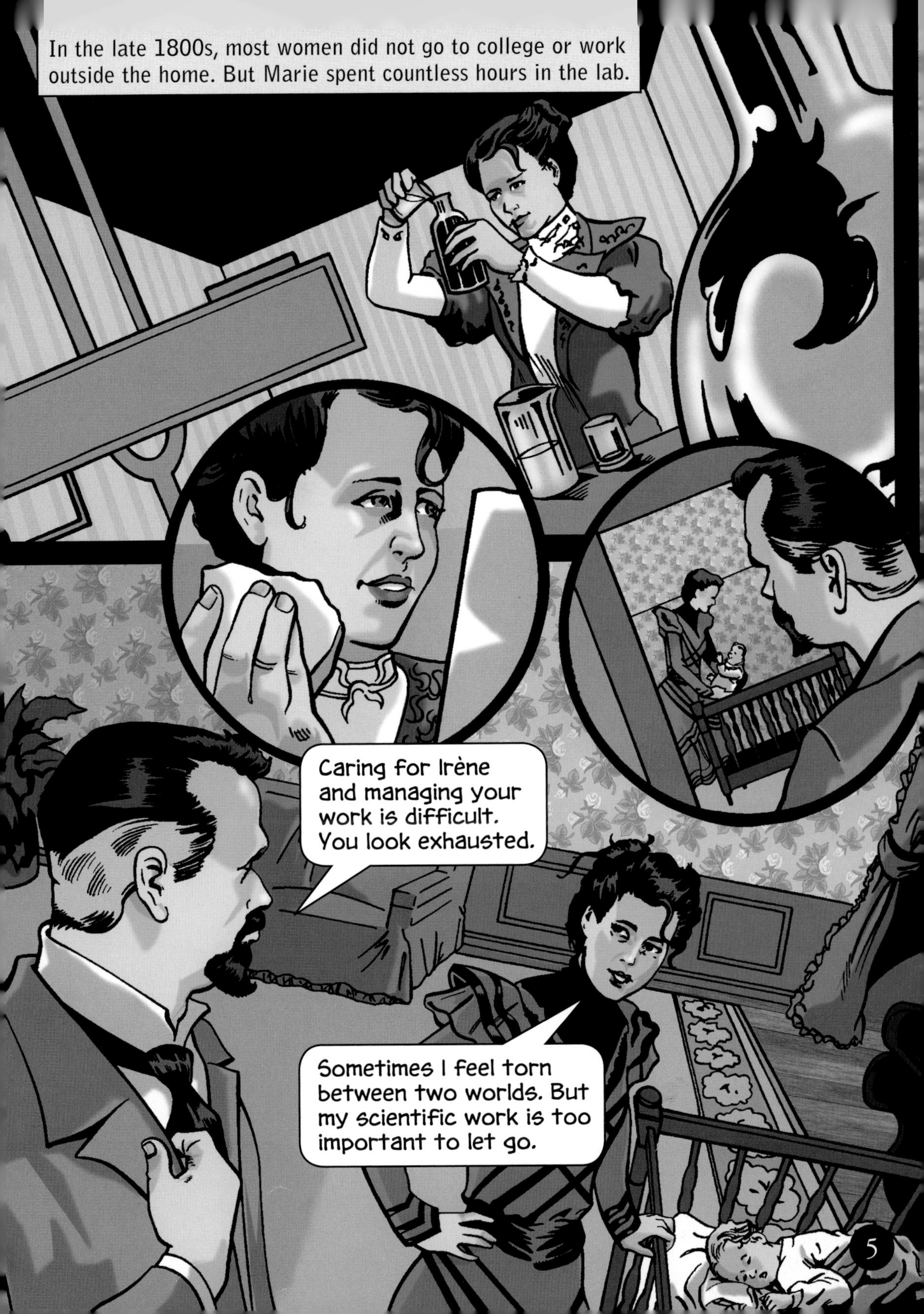
In the late 1800s, most women did not go to college or work outside the home. But Marie spent countless hours in the lab.
Caring for Irène and managing your work is difficult. You look exhausted.
Sometimes I feel torn between two worlds. But my scientific work is too important to let go.

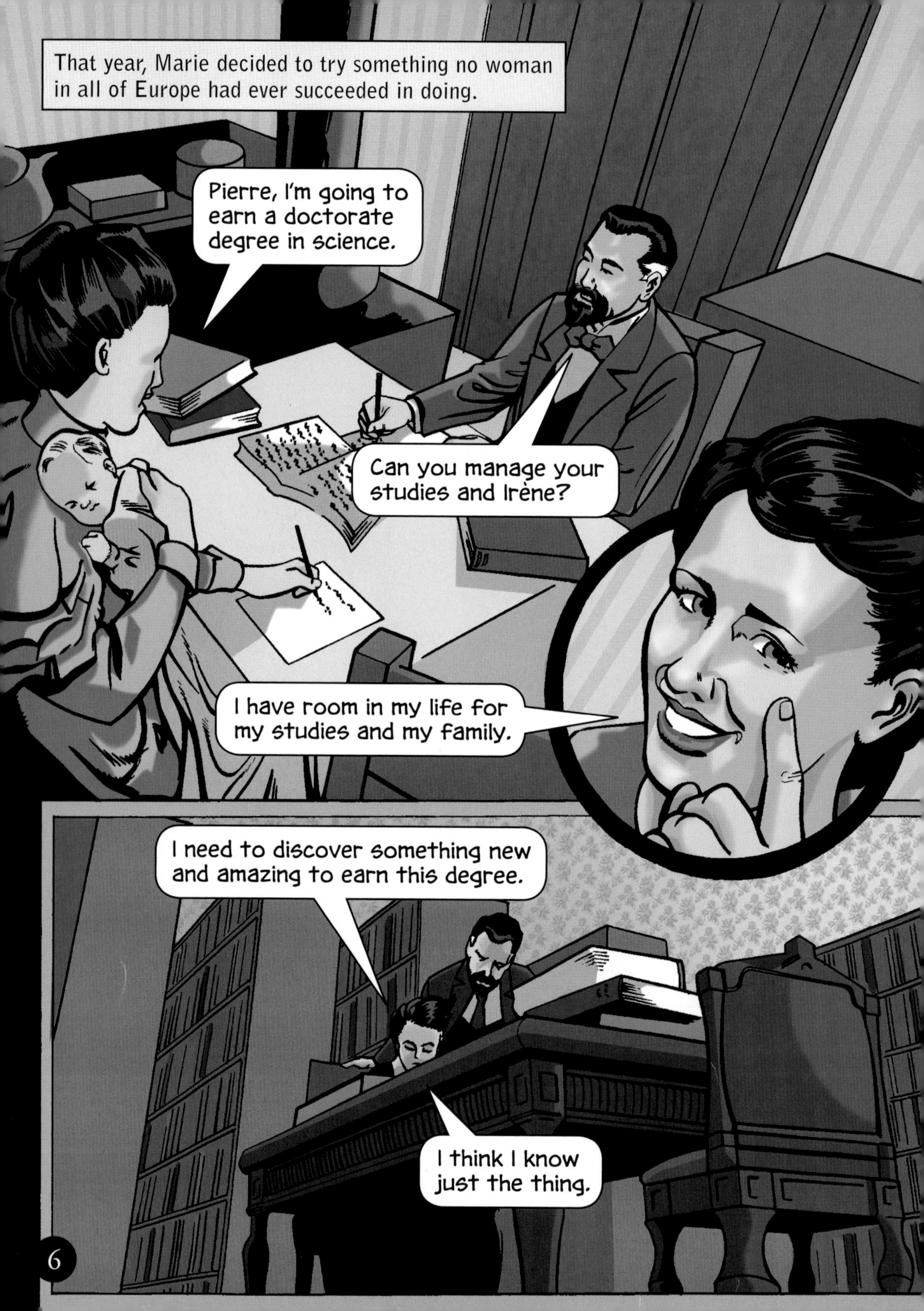
That year, Marie decided to try something no woman in all of Europe had ever succeeded in doing.
Pierre, I'm going to earn a doctorate degree in science.
Can you manage your studies and Irène?
I have room in my life for my studies and my family.
I need to discover something new and amazing to earn this degree.
I think I know just the thing.

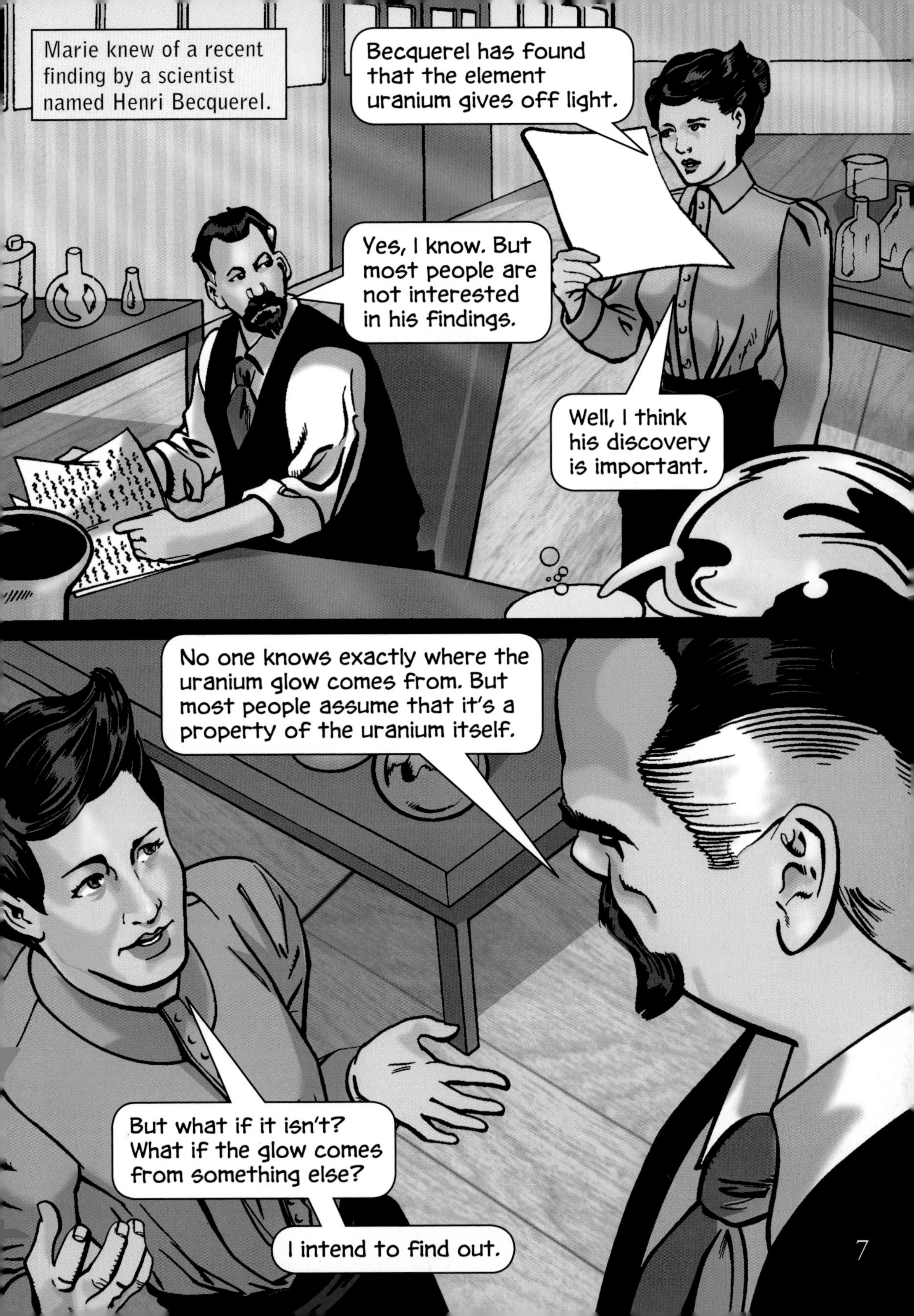
Marie knew of a recent finding by a scientist named Henri Becquerel.
Becquerel has found that the element uranium gives off light.
Yes, I know. But most people are not interested in his findings.
Well, I think his discovery is important.
No one knows exactly where the uranium glow comes from. But most people assume that it's a property of the uranium itself.
But what if it isn't? What if the glow comes from something else?
I intend to find out.

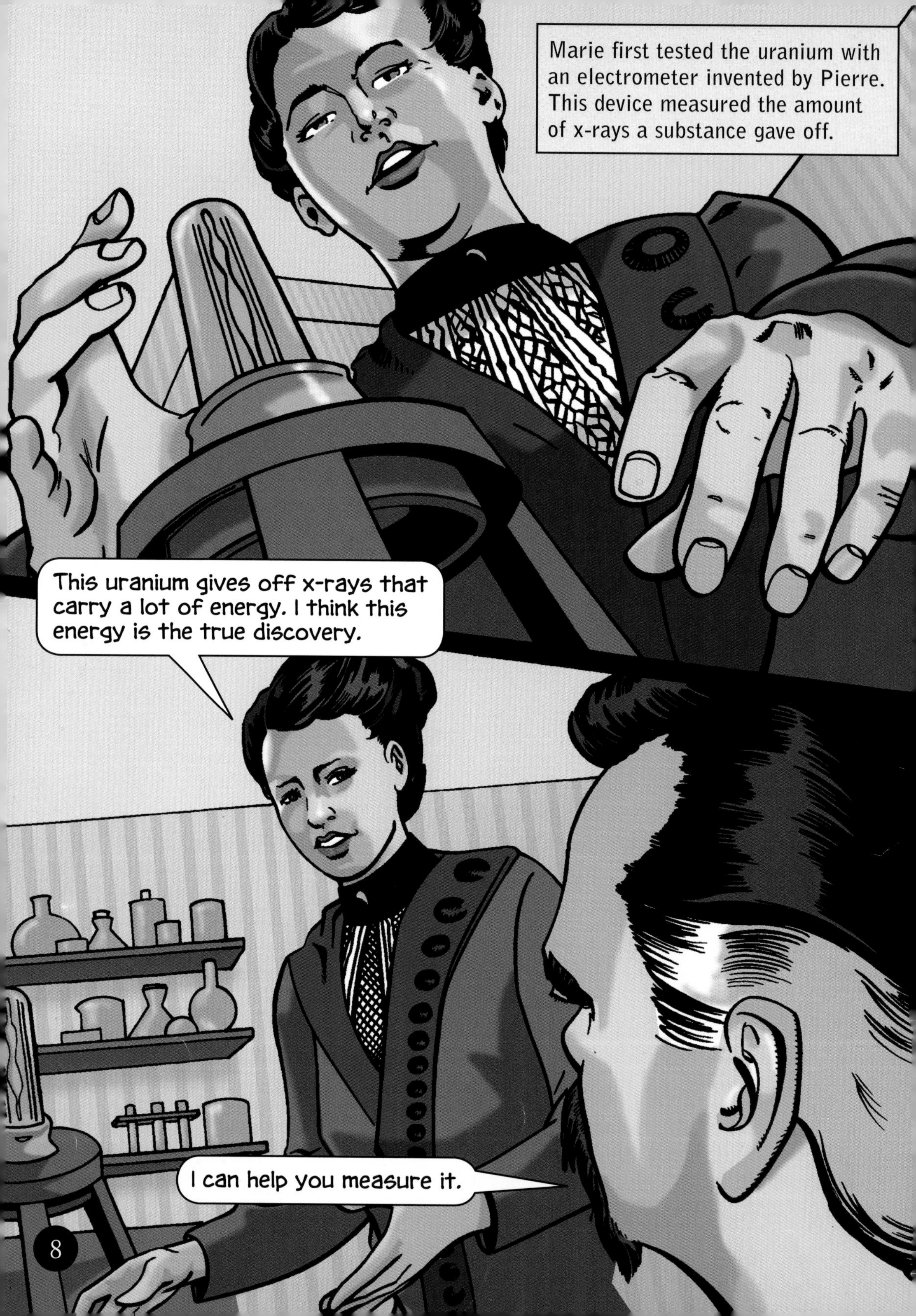

Marie first tested the uranium with an electrometer invented by Pierre. This device measured the amount of x-rays a substance gave off.
This uranium gives off x-rays that carry a lot of energy. I think this energy is the true discovery.
I can help you measure it.

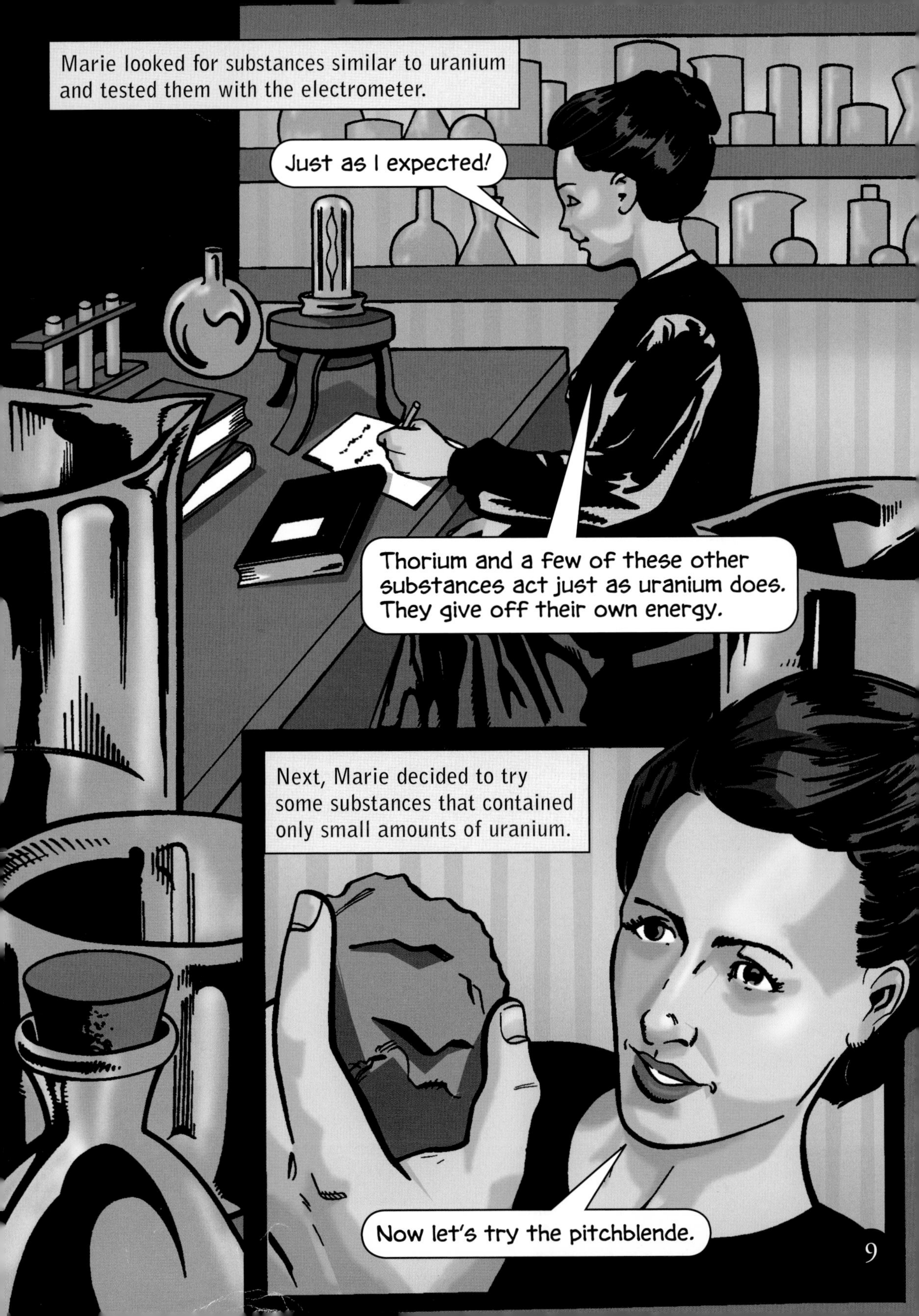
Marie looked for substances similar to uranium and tested them with the electrometer.
Just as I expected!
Thorium and a few of these other substances act just as uranium does. They give off their own energy.
Next, Marie decided to try some substances that contained only small amounts of uranium.
Now let's try the pitchblende.

CHAPTER 2
THE DISCOVERY

Pitchblende was considered mine waste after the uranium was removed. Mine owners were happy to give it to the Curies for their experiments. Only a very small amount of uranium remained in the pitchblende.

Look at these readings, Pierre. I expected the pitchblende to give out less energy than pure uranium. But it has more.

There must be some mistake. Let's test it again.

I have already retested it.

This can only mean one thing.

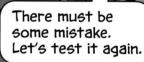

A new element is giving off all that energy!

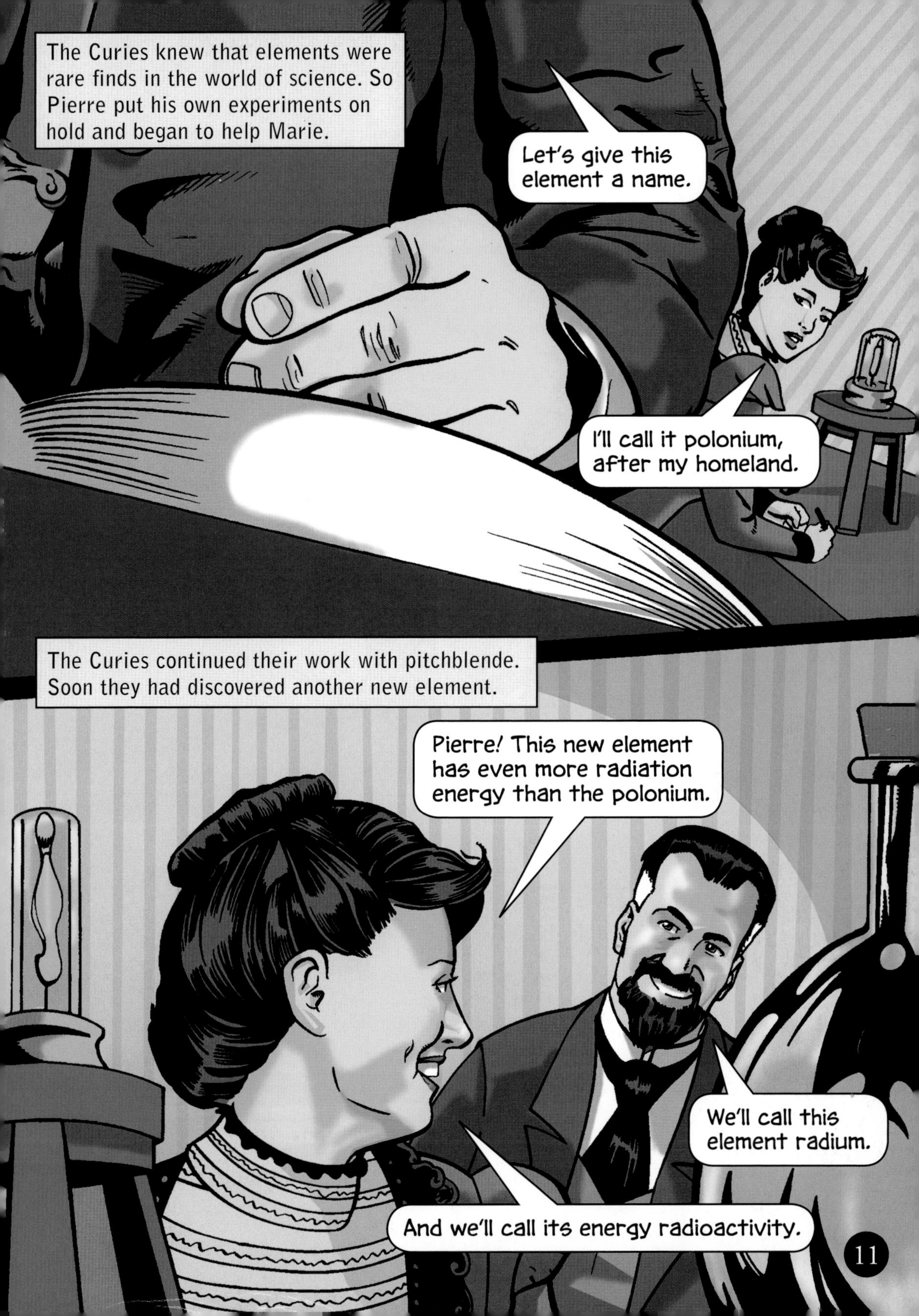
The Curies knew that elements were rare finds in the world of science. So Pierre put his own experiments on hold and began to help Marie.
Let's give this element a name.
I'll call it polonium, after my homeland.
The Curies continued their work with pitchblende. Soon they had discovered another new element.
Pierre! This new element has even more radiation energy than the polonium.
We'll call this element radium.
And we'll call its energy radioactivity.

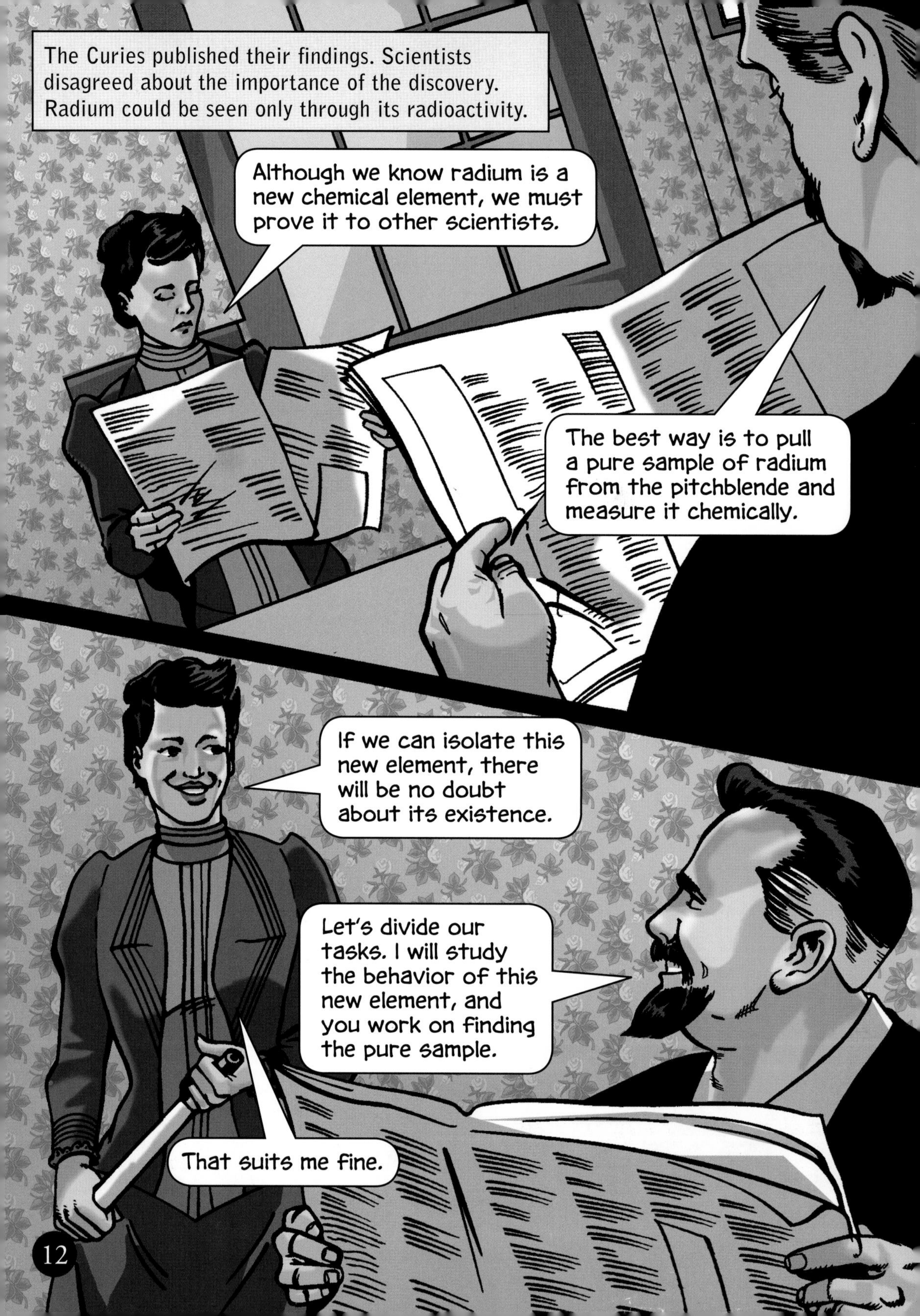
The Curies published their findings. Scientists disagreed about the importance of the discovery. Radium could be seen only through its radioactivity.
Although we know radium is a new chemical element, we must prove it to other scientists.
The best way is to pull a pure sample of radium from the pitchblende and measure it chemically.
If we can isolate this new element, there will be no doubt about its existence.
Let's divide our tasks. I will study the behavior of this new element, and you work on finding the pure sample.
That suits me fine.

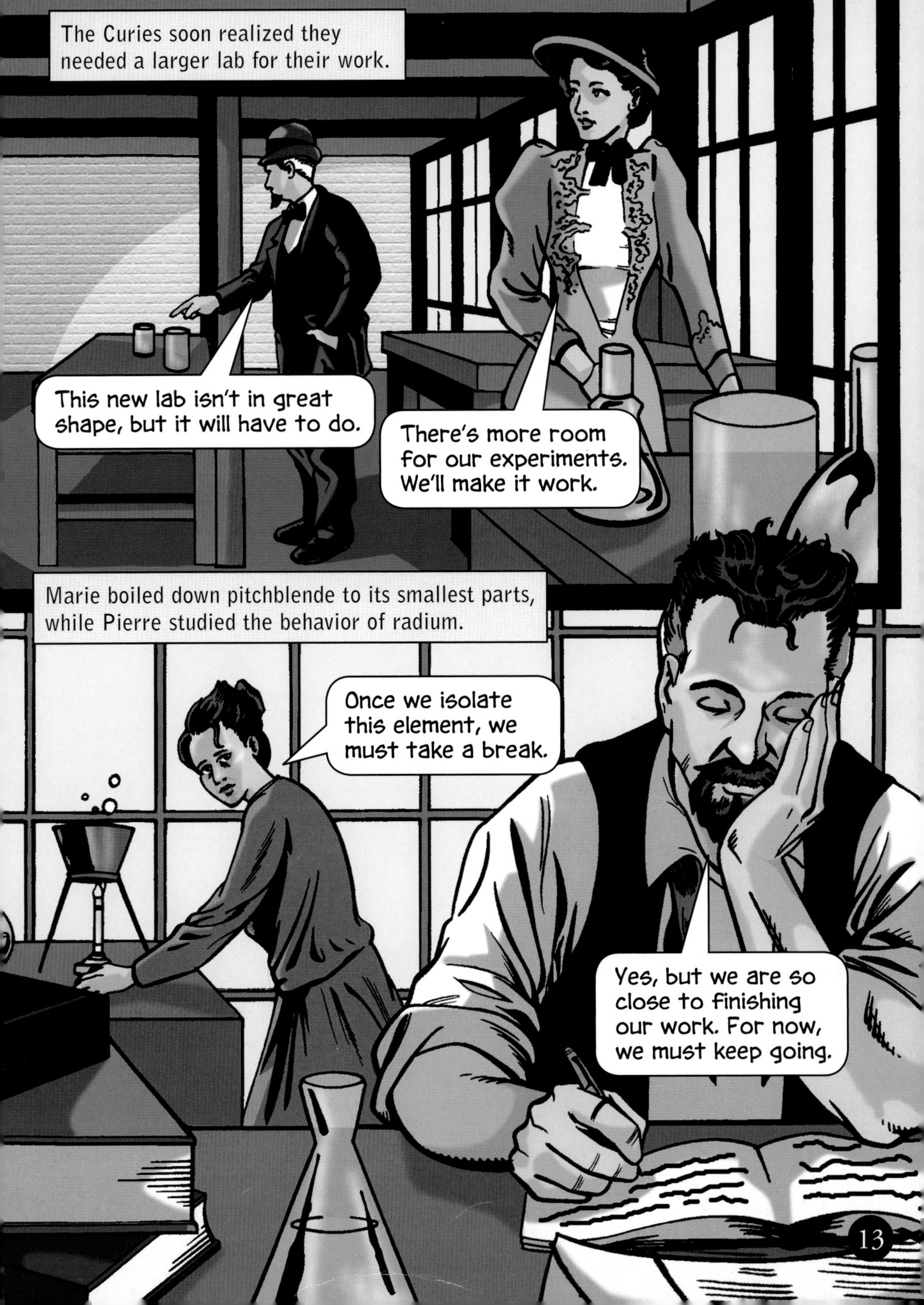
The Curies soon realized they needed a larger lab for their work.
This new lab isn't in great shape, but it will have to do.
There's more room for our experiments. We'll make it work.
Marie boiled down pitchblende to its smallest parts, while Pierre studied the behavior of radium.
Once we isolate this element, we must take a break.
Yes, but we are so close to finishing our work. For now, we must keep going.

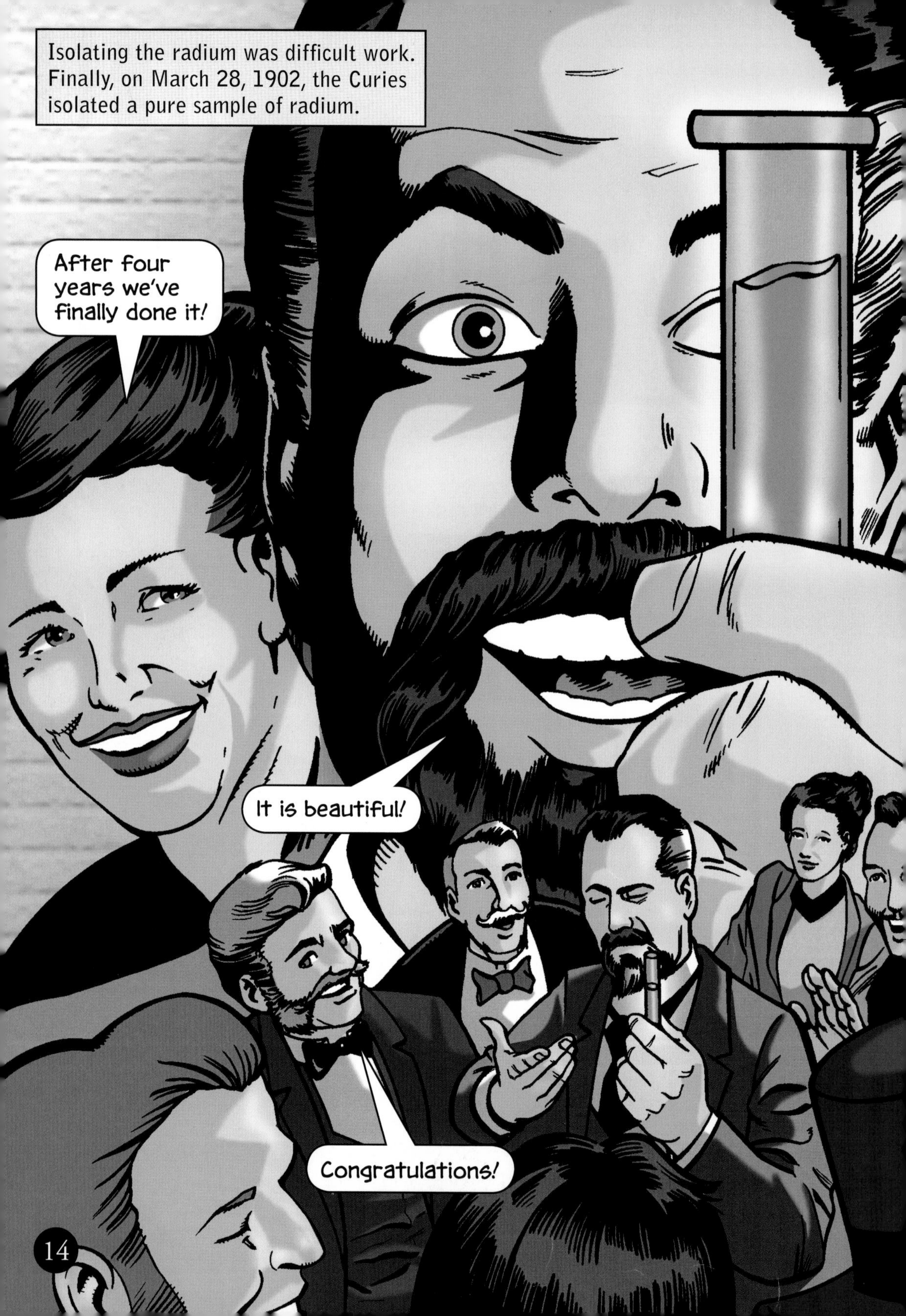
Isolating the radium was difficult work. Finally, on March 28, 1902, the Curies isolated a pure sample of radium.
After four years we've finally done it!
It is beautiful!
Congratulations!

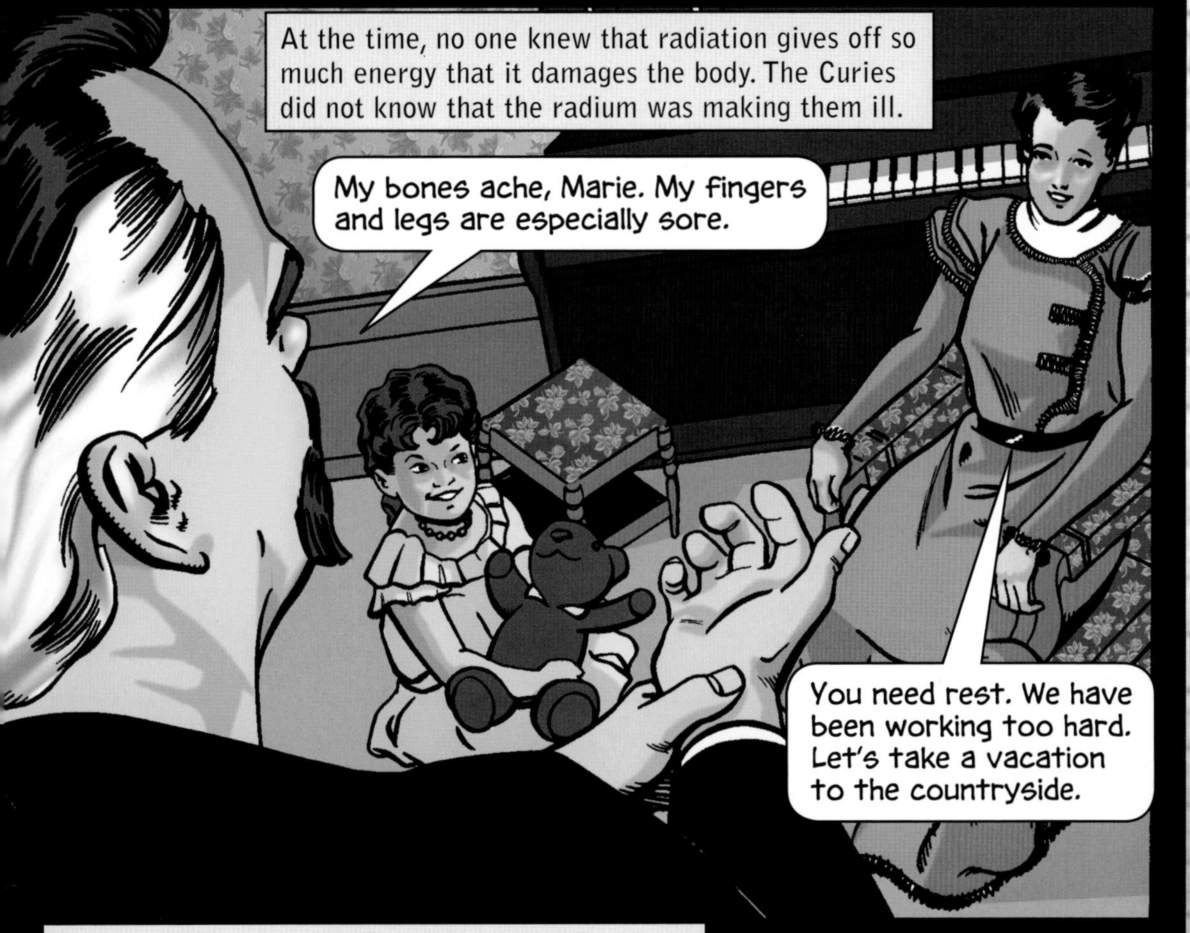
At the time, no one knew that radiation gives off so much energy that it damages the body. The Curies did not know that the radium was making them ill.
My bones ache, Marie. My fingers and legs are especially sore.
You need rest. We have been working too hard. Let's take a vacation to the countryside.

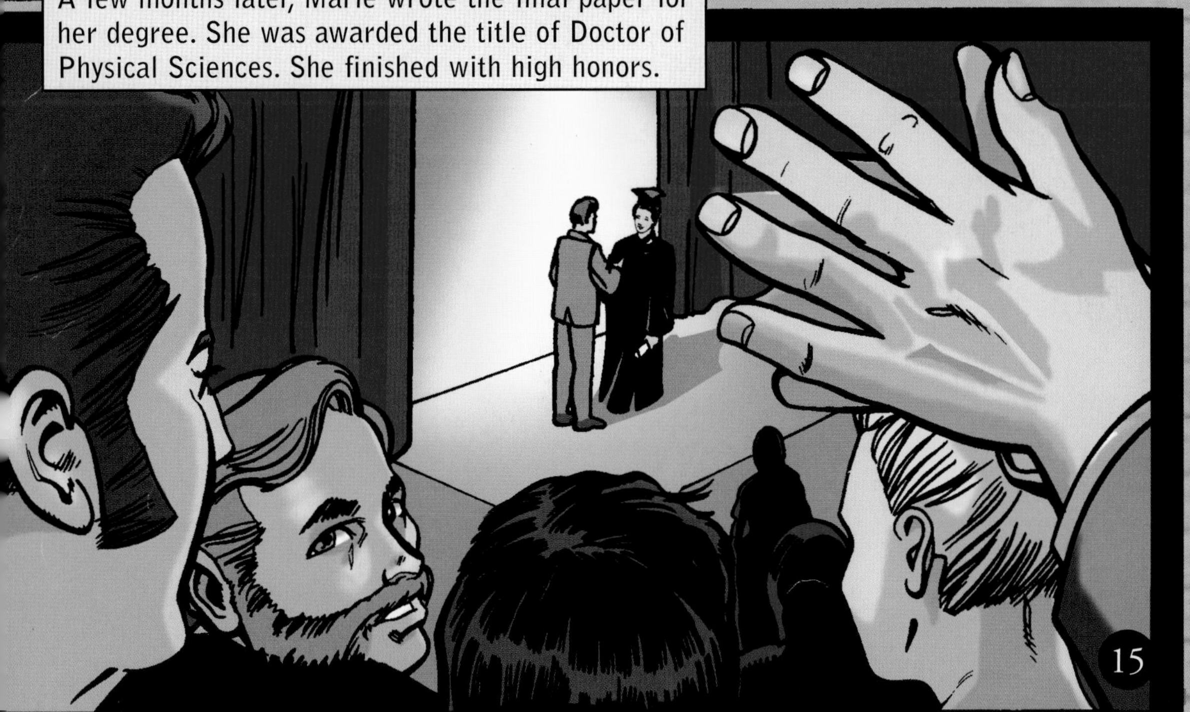
A few months later, Marie wrote the final paper for her degree. She was awarded the title of Doctor of Physical Sciences. She finished with high honors.

Chapter 3
Radium and Radiation Therapy

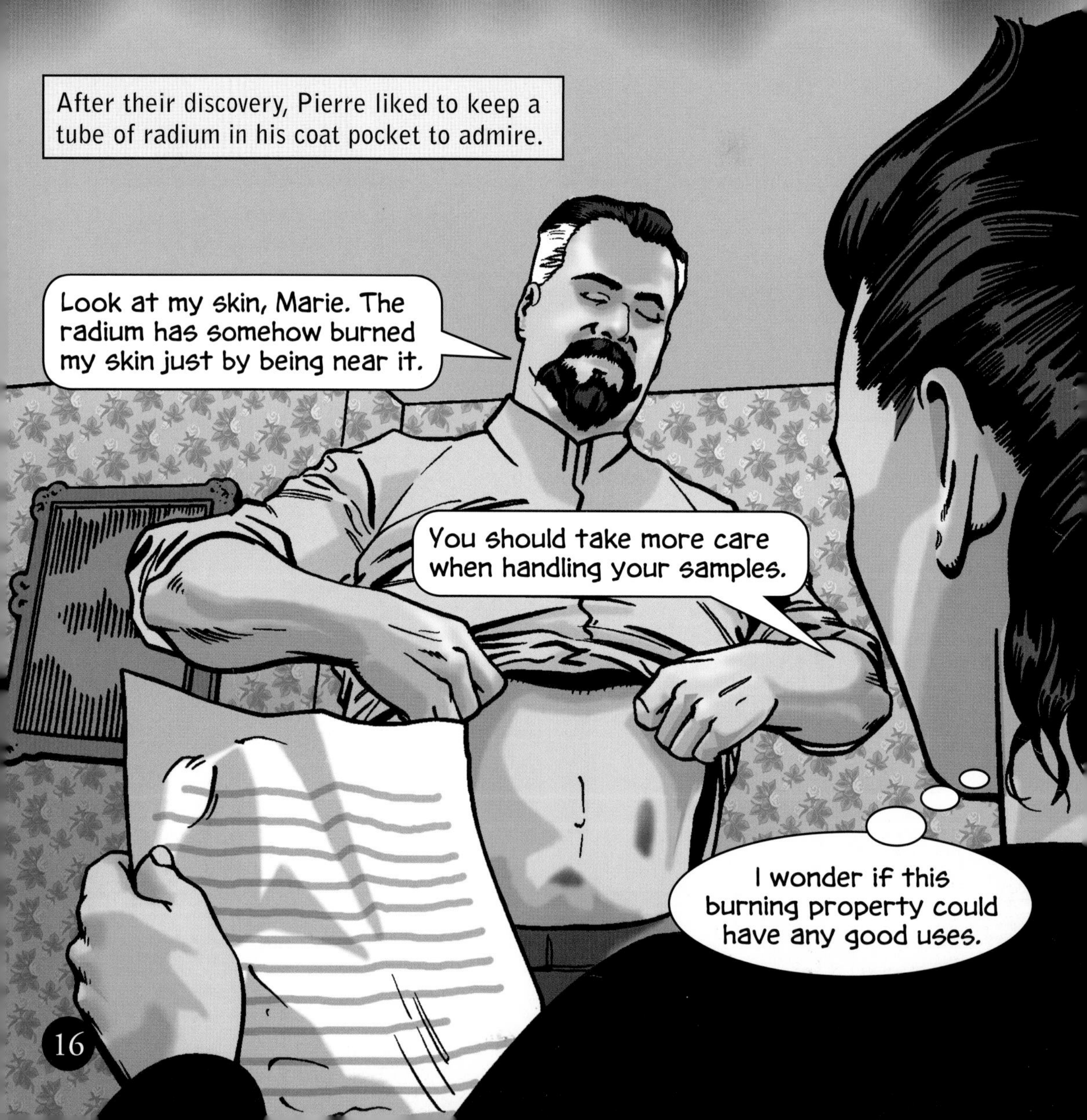

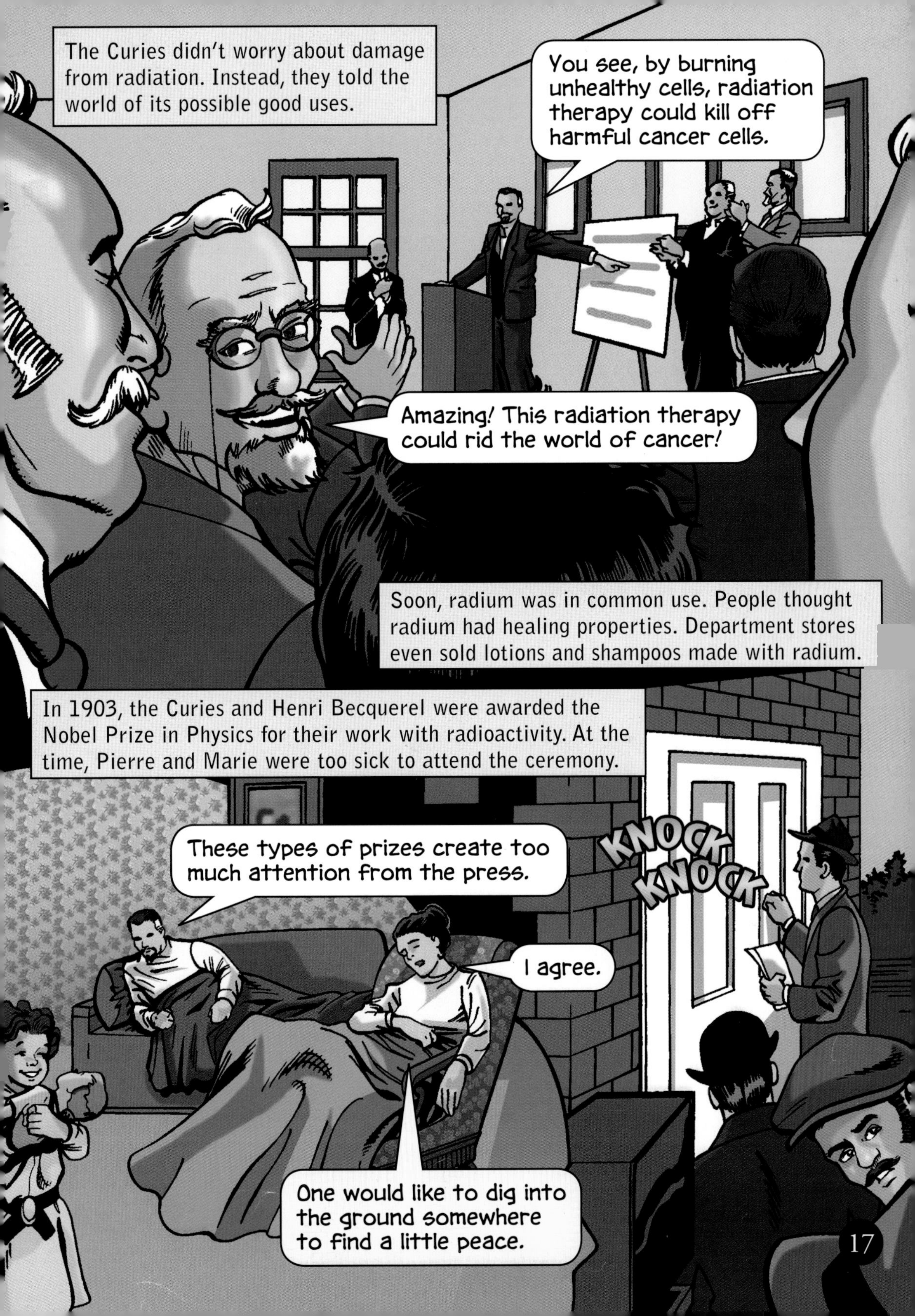
The Curies didn't worry about damage from radiation. Instead, they told the world of its possible good uses.
You see, by burning unhealthy cells, radiation therapy could kill off harmful cancer cells.
Amazing! This radiation therapy could rid the world of cancer!
Soon, radium was in common use. People thought radium had healing properties. Department stores even sold lotions and shampoos made with radium.
In 1903, the Curies and Henri Becquerel were awarded the Nobel Prize in Physics for their work with radioactivity. At the time, Pierre and Marie were too sick to attend the ceremony.
These types of prizes create too much attention from the press.
KNOCK KNOCK
I agree.
One would like to dig into the ground somewhere to find a little peace.

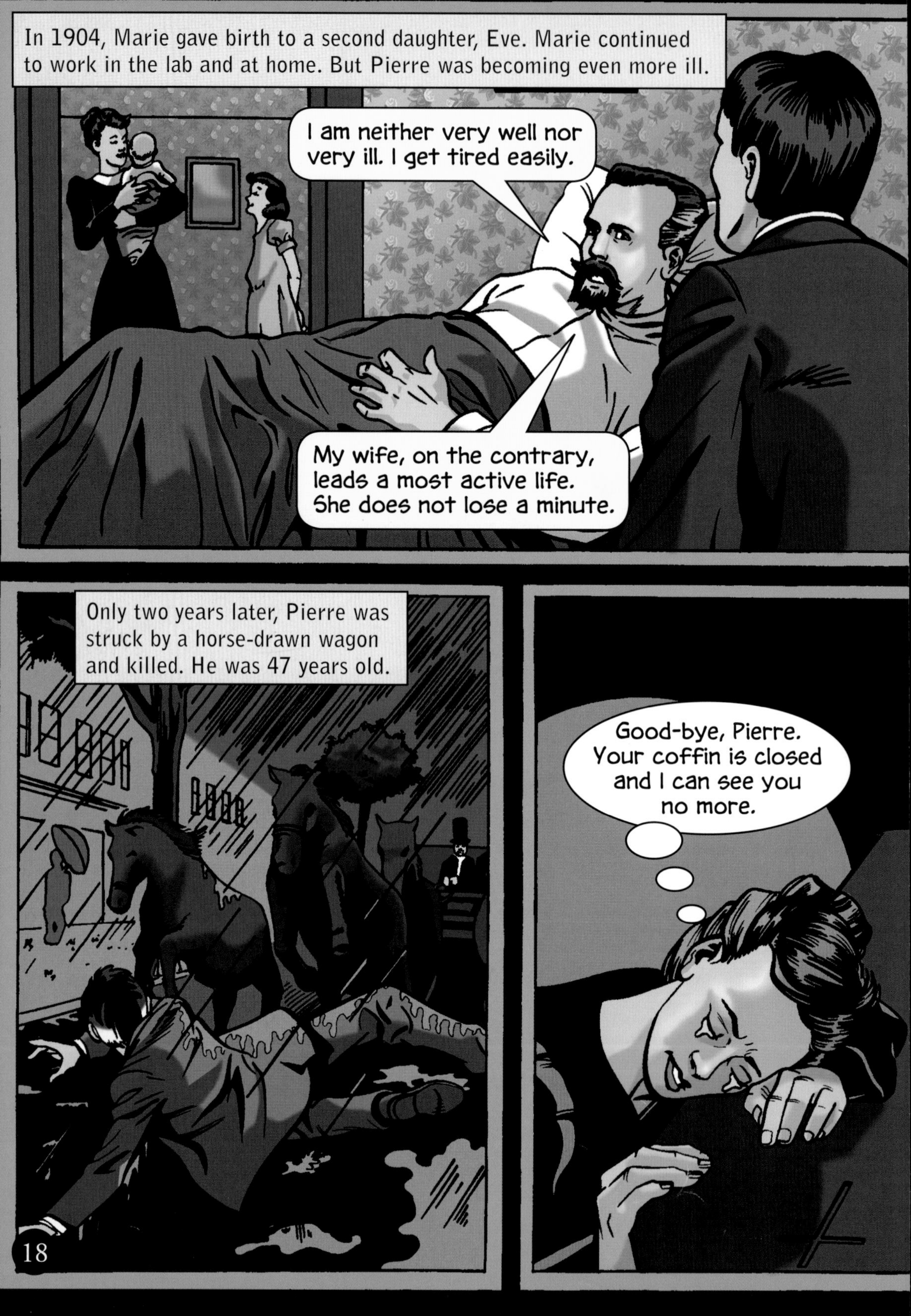
In 1904, Marie gave birth to a second daughter, Eve. Marie continued to work in the lab and at home. But Pierre was becoming even more ill.
I am neither very well nor very ill. I get tired easily.
My wife, on the contrary, leads a most active life. She does not lose a minute.
Only two years later, Pierre was struck by a horse-drawn wagon and killed. He was 47 years old.
Good-bye, Pierre. Your coffin is closed and I can see you no more.

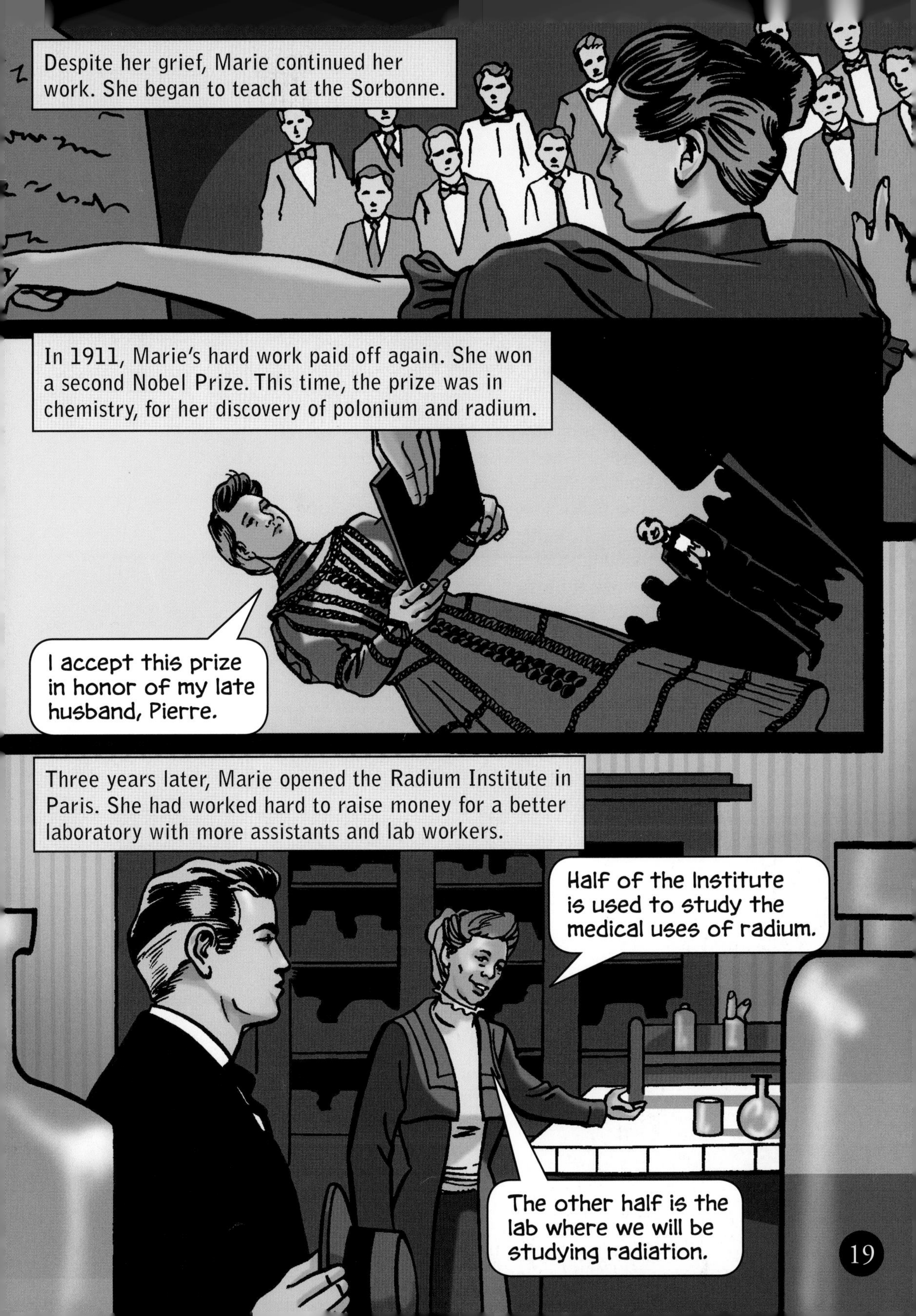
Despite her grief, Marie continued her work. She began to teach at the Sorbonne.
In 1911, Marie's hard work paid off again. She won a second Nobel Prize. This time, the prize was in chemistry, for her discovery of polonium and radium.
I accept this prize in honor of my late husband, Pierre.
Three years later, Marie opened the Radium Institute in Paris. She had worked hard to raise money for a better laboratory with more assistants and lab workers.
Half of the Institute is used to study the medical uses of radium.
The other half is the lab where we will be studying radiation.

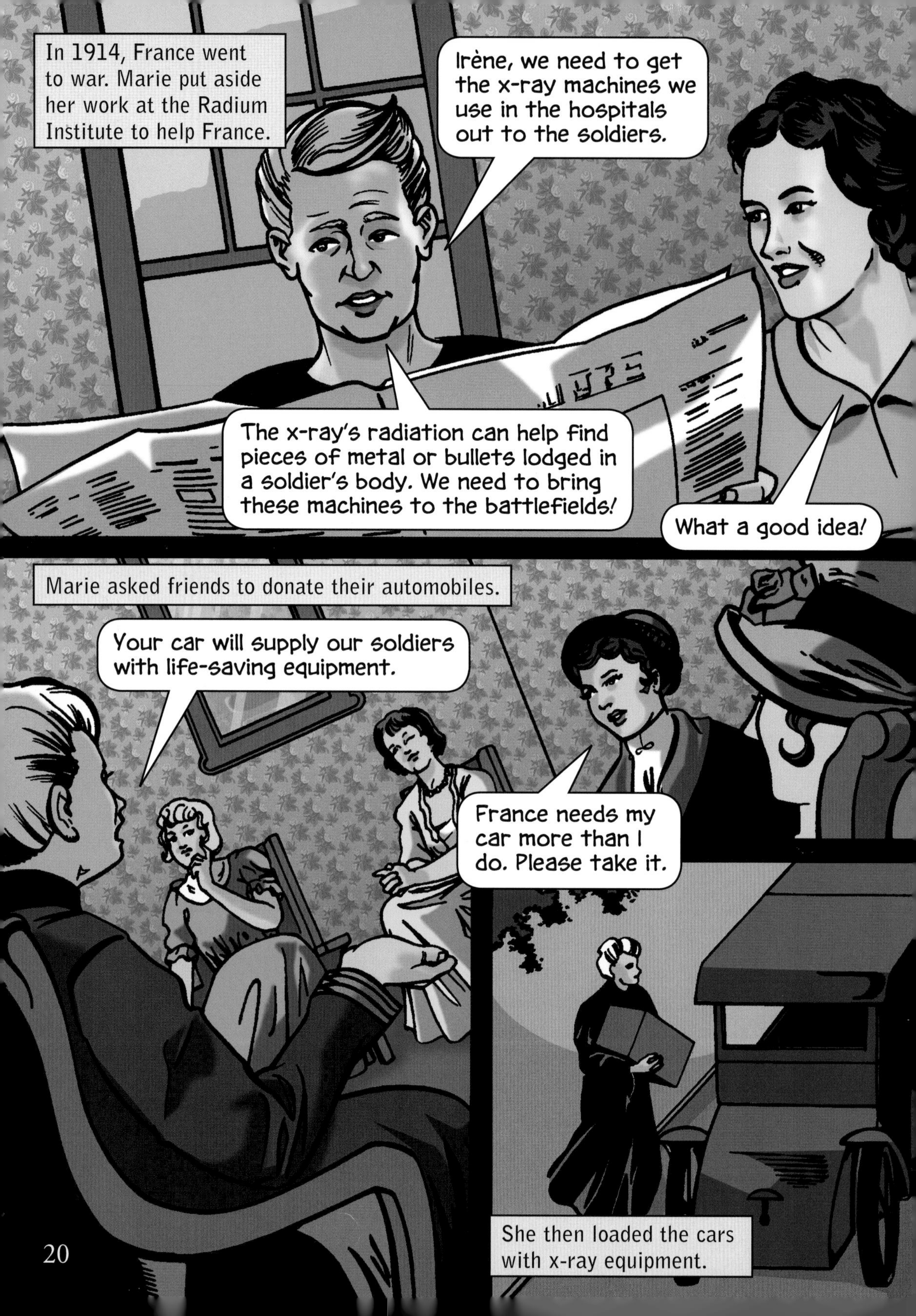
In 1914, France went to war. Marie put aside her work at the Radium Institute to help France.
Irène, we need to get the x-ray machines we use in the hospitals out to the soldiers.
The x-ray's radiation can help find pieces of metal or bullets lodged in a soldier's body. We need to bring these machines to the battlefields!
What a good idea!
Marie asked friends to donate their automobiles.
Your car will supply our soldiers with life-saving equipment.
France needs my car more than I do. Please take it.
She then loaded the cars with x-ray equipment.

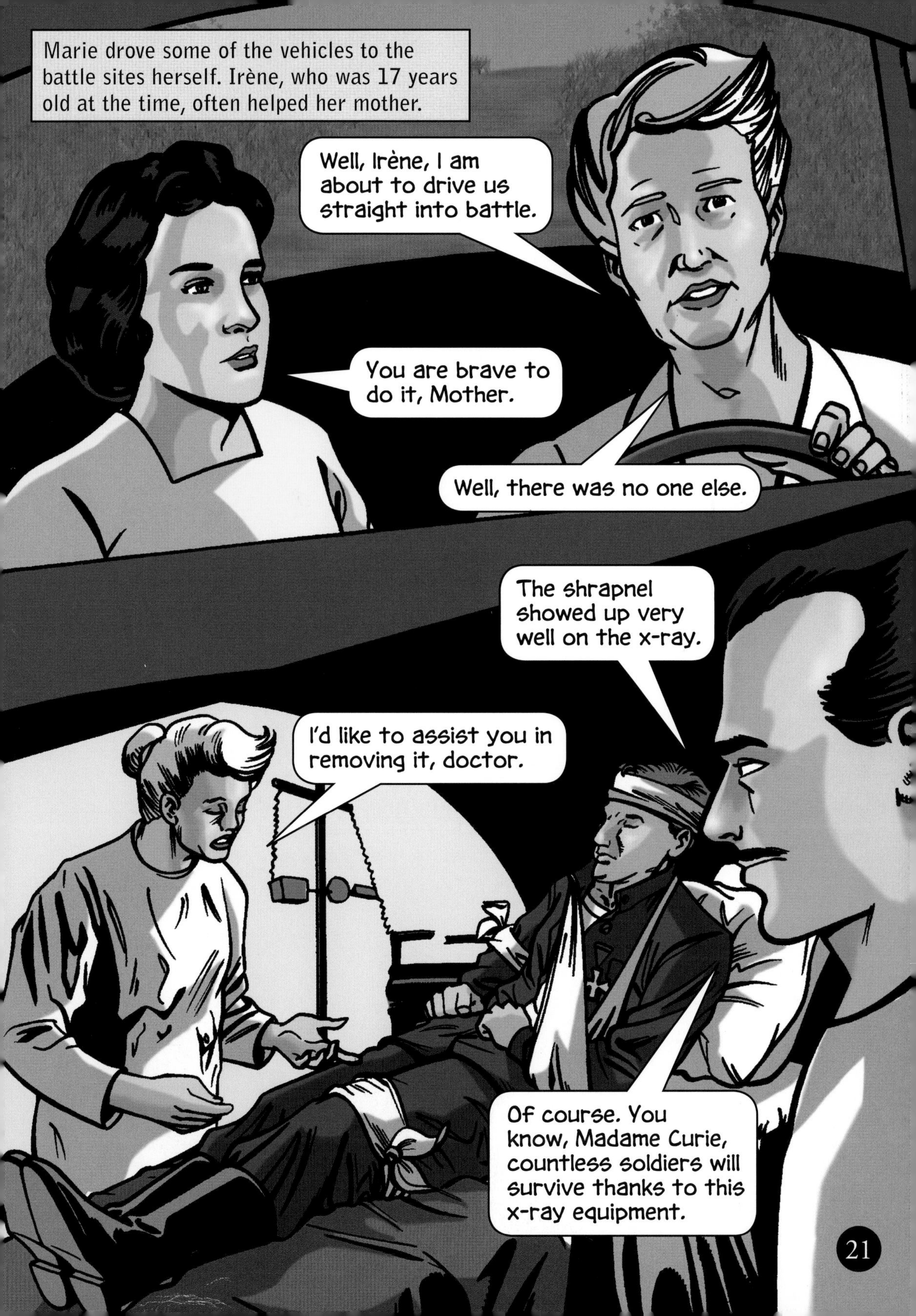
Marie drove some of the vehicles to the battle sites herself. Irène, who was 17 years old at the time, often helped her mother.
Well, Irène, I am about to drive us straight into battle.
You are brave to do it, Mother.
Well, there was no one else.
The shrapnel showed up very well on the x-ray.
I'd like to assist you in removing it, doctor.
Of course. You know, Madame Curie, countless soldiers will survive thanks to this x-ray equipment.

Chapter 4
The Curie Legacy

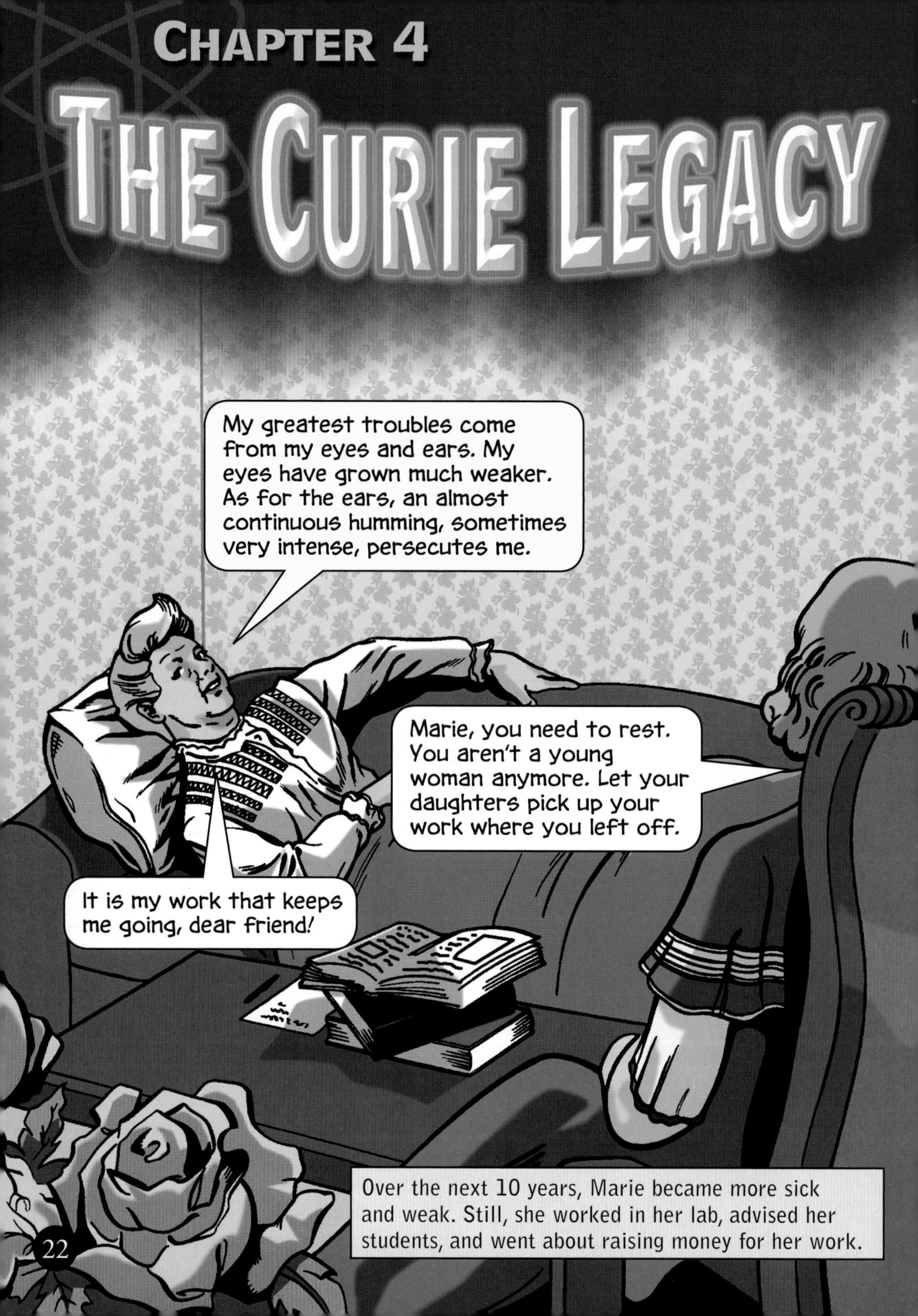
My greatest troubles come from my eyes and ears. My eyes have grown much weaker. As for the ears, an almost continuous humming, sometimes very intense, persecutes me.
Marie, you need to rest. You aren't a young woman anymore. Let your daughters pick up your work where you left off.
It is my work that keeps me going, dear friend!
Over the next 10 years, Marie became more sick and weak. Still, she worked in her lab, advised her students, and went about raising money for her work.

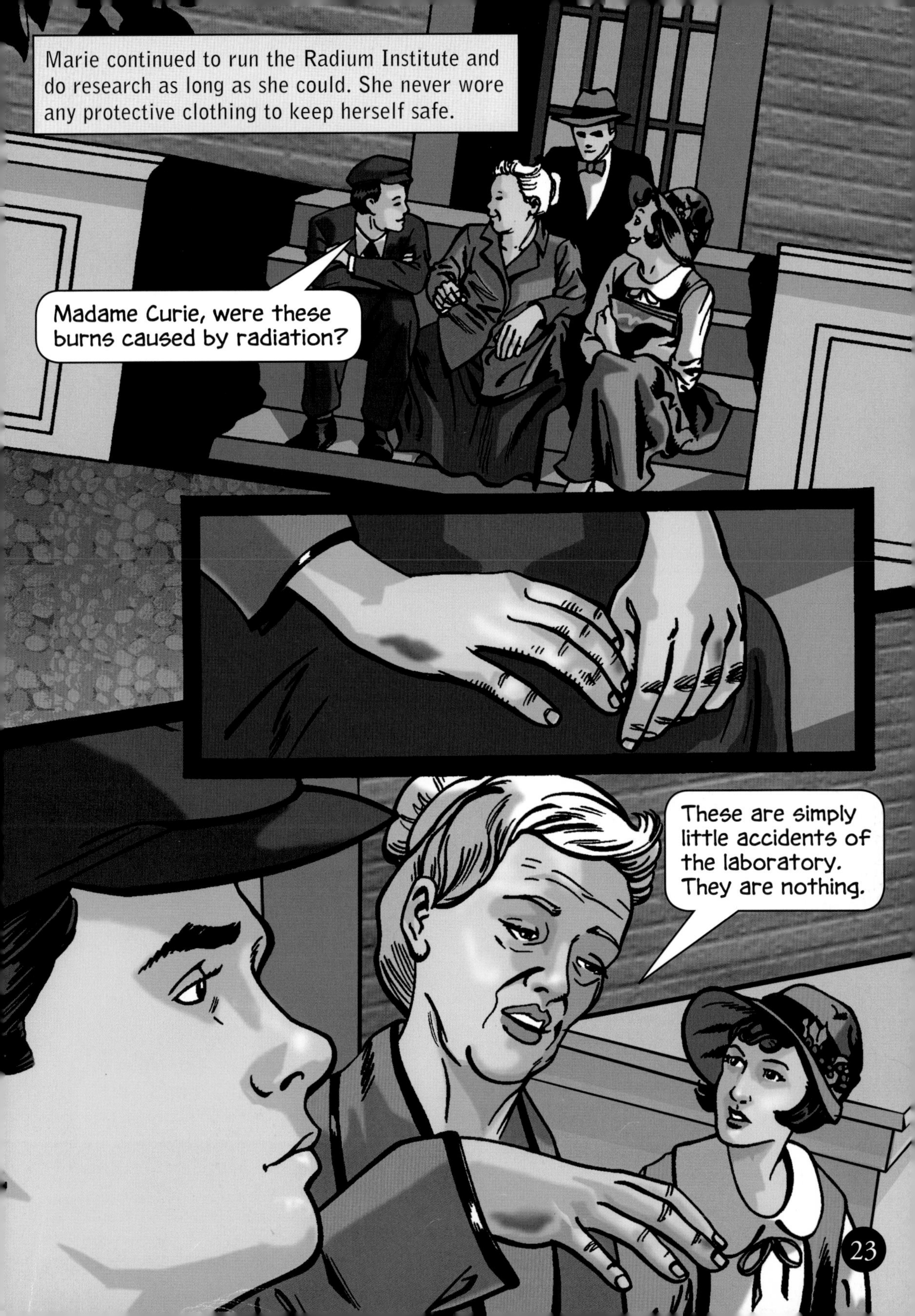
Marie continued to run the Radium Institute and do research as long as she could. She never wore any protective clothing to keep herself safe.
Madame Curie, were these burns caused by radiation?
These are simply little accidents of the laboratory. They are nothing.

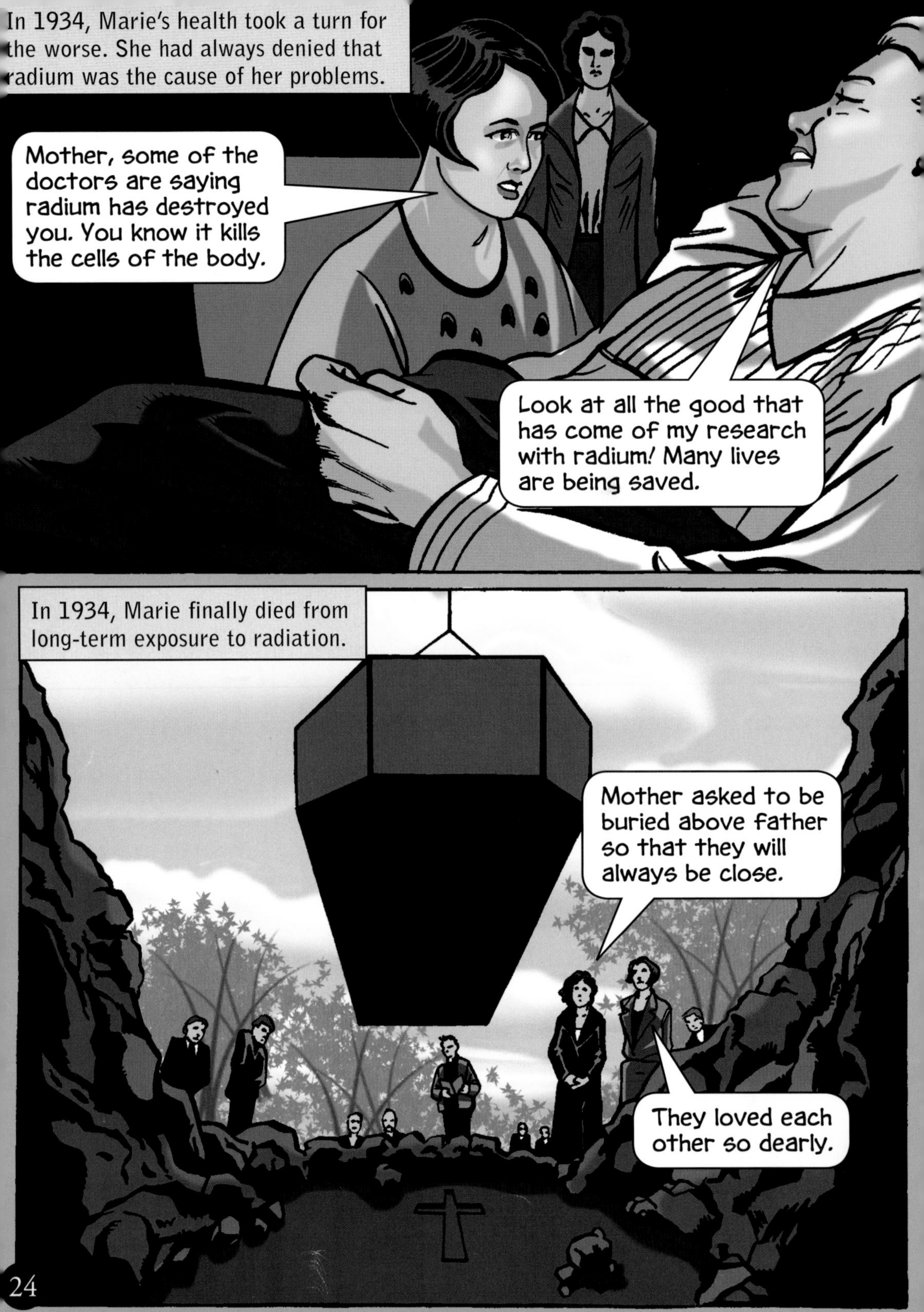
In 1934, Marie's health took a turn for the worse. She had always denied that radium was the cause of her problems.
Mother, some of the doctors are saying radium has destroyed you. You know it kills the cells of the body.
Look at all the good that has come of my research with radium! Many lives are being saved.
In 1934, Marie finally died from long-term exposure to radiation.
Mother asked to be buried above father so that they will always be close.
They loved each other so dearly.

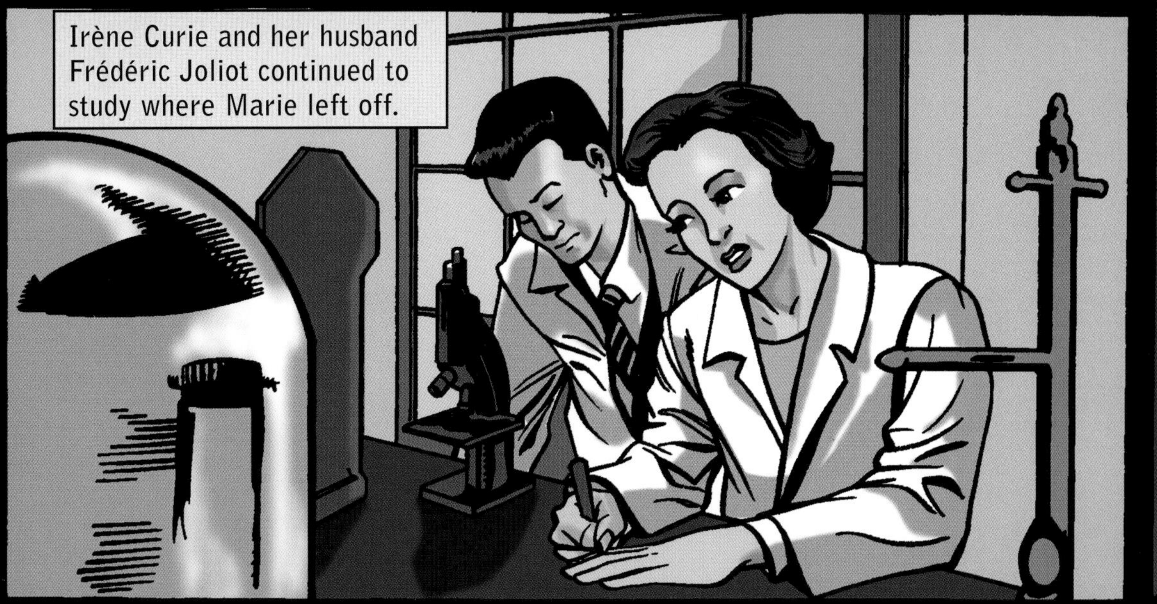
Irène Curie and her husband Frédéric Joliot continued to study where Marie left off.

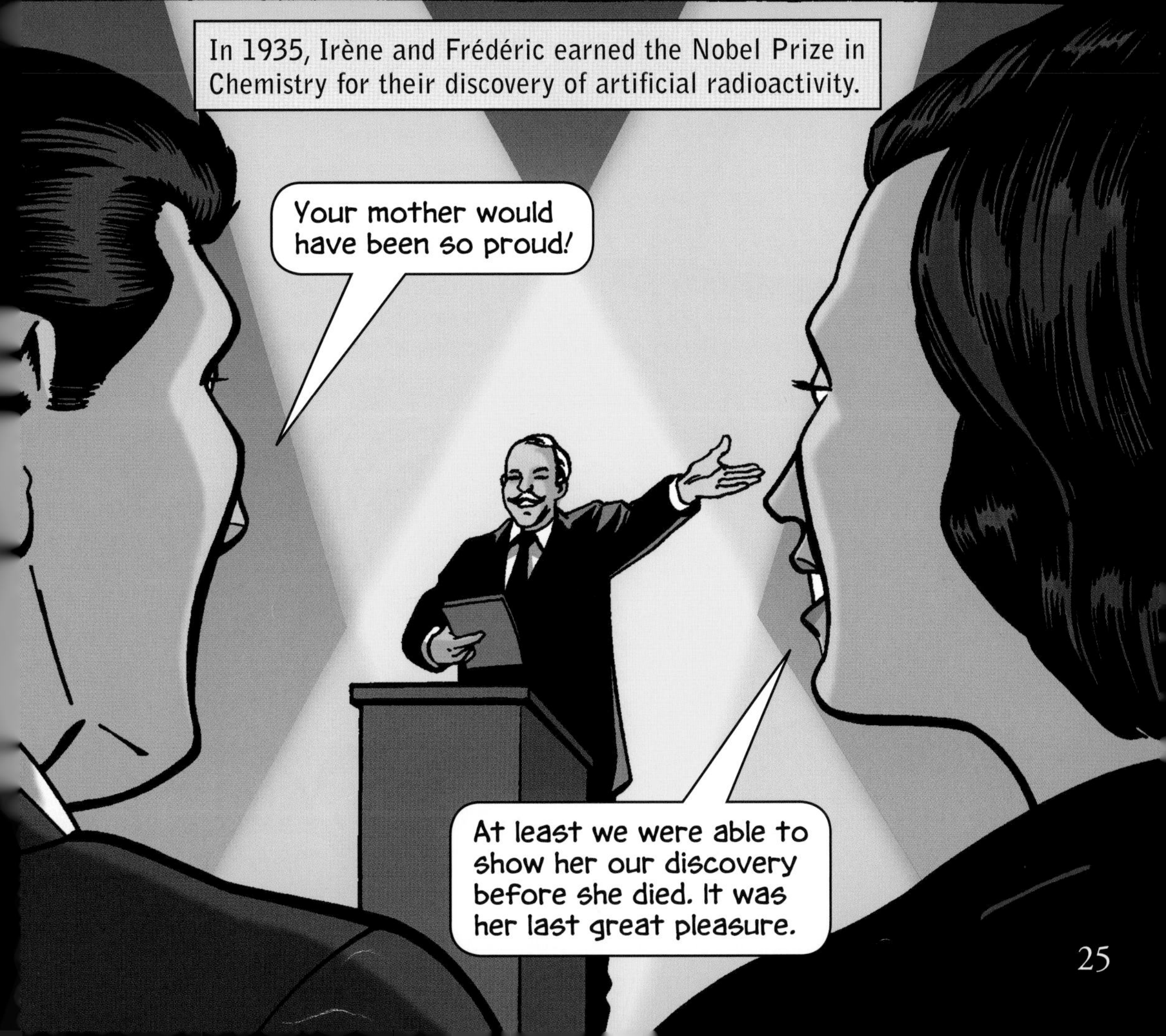
In 1935, Irène and Frédéric earned the Nobel Prize in Chemistry for their discovery of artificial radioactivity.
Your mother would have been so proud!
At least we were able to show her our discovery before she died. It was her last great pleasure.

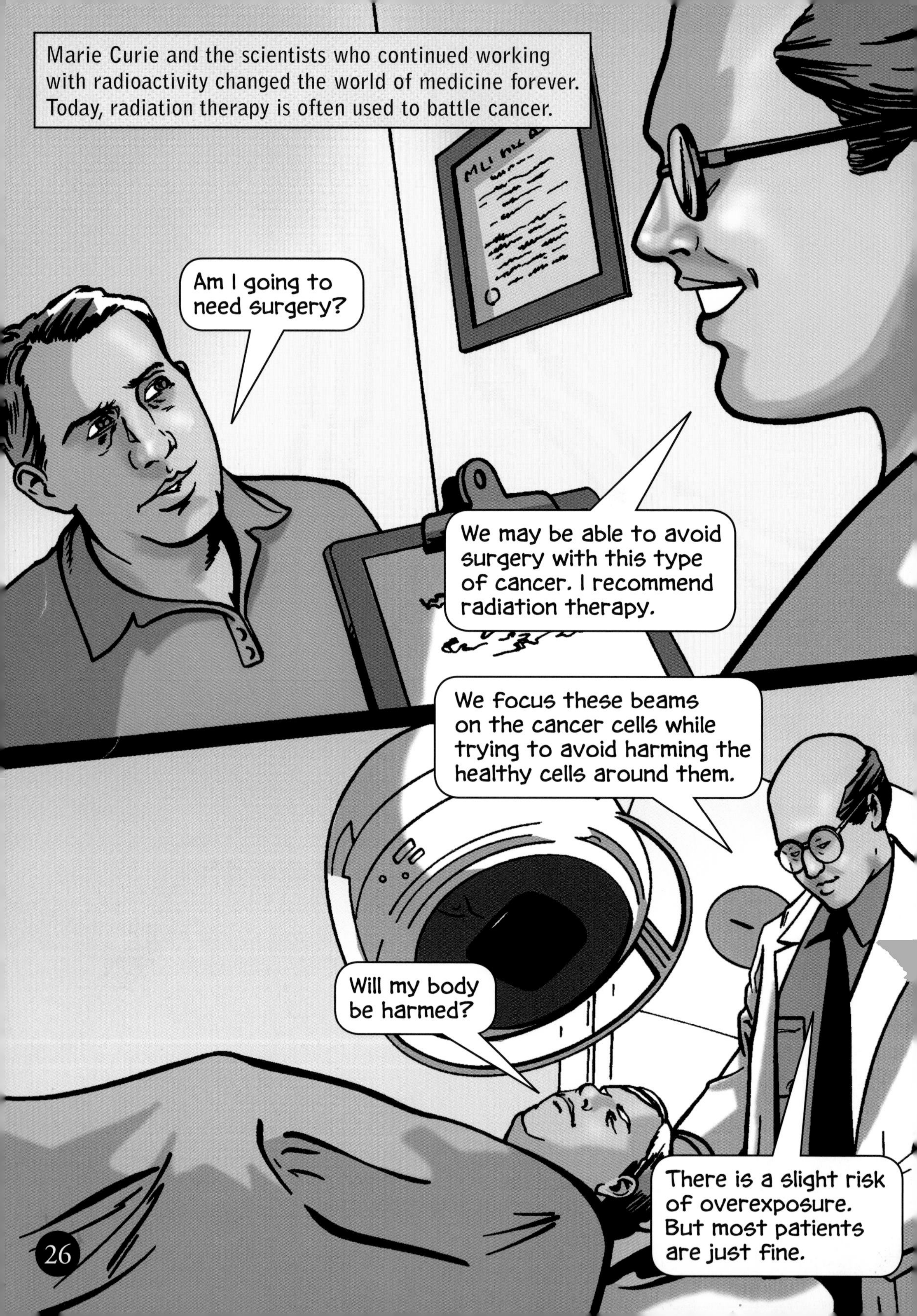
Marie Curie and the scientists who continued working with radioactivity changed the world of medicine forever. Today, radiation therapy is often used to battle cancer.
Am I going to need surgery?
We may be able to avoid surgery with this type of cancer. I recommend radiation therapy.
We focus these beams on the cancer cells while trying to avoid harming the healthy cells around them.
Will my body be harmed?
There is a slight risk of overexposure. But most patients are just fine.

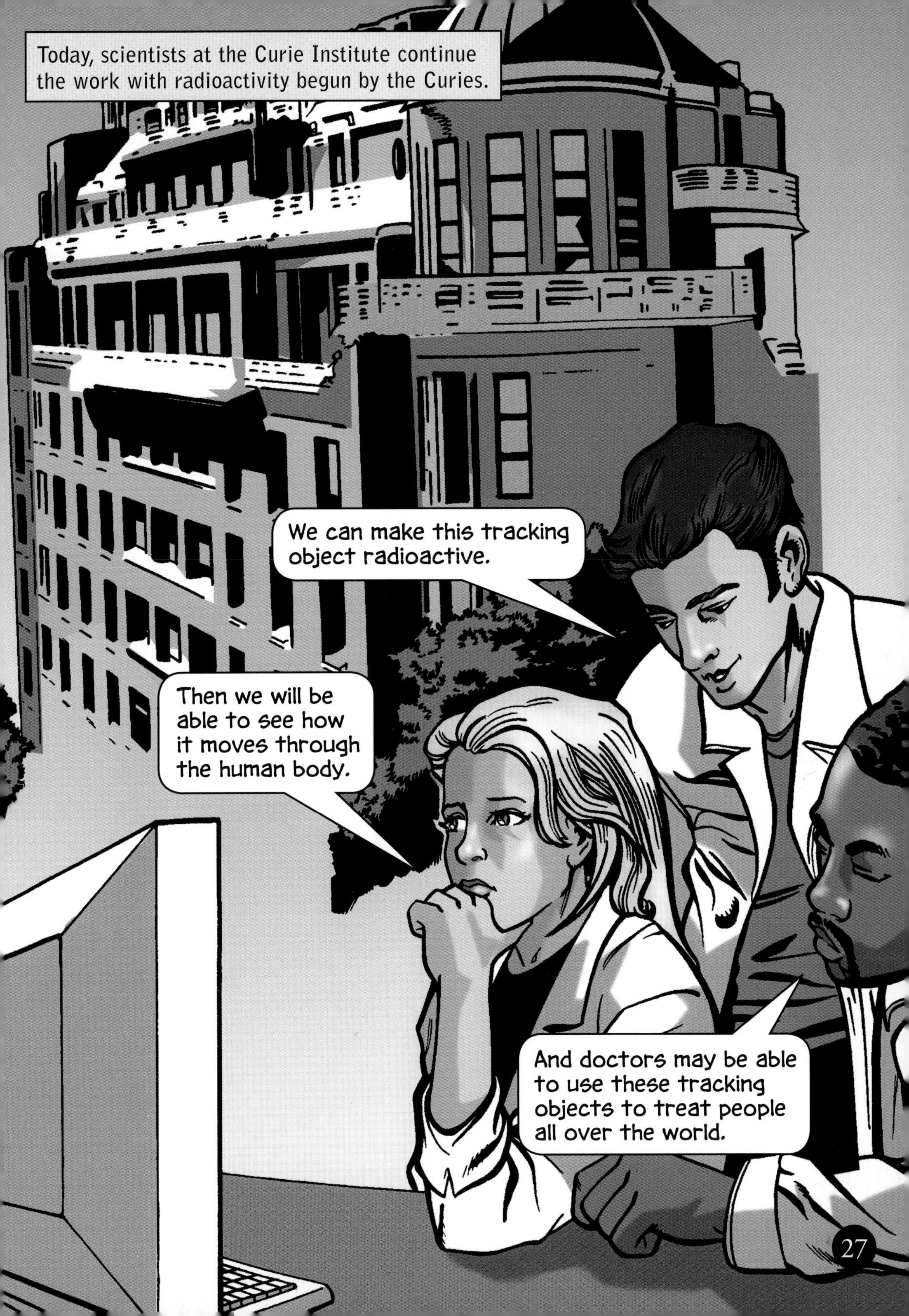
Today, scientists at the Curie Institute continue the work with radioactivity begun by the Curies.
We can make this tracking object radioactive.
Then we will be able to see how it moves through the human body.
And doctors may be able to use these tracking objects to treat people all over the world.

MORE ABOUT
MARIE ✳ CURIE AND
RADIOACTIVITY

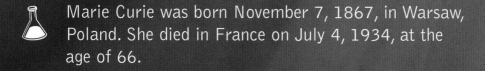
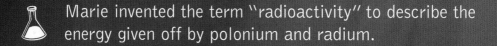

Marie Curie was born November 7, 1867, in Warsaw, Poland. She died in France on July 4, 1934, at the age of 66.

Marie invented the term "radioactivity" to describe the energy given off by polonium and radium.

Marie took good notes in her laboratory notebooks while doing research on radium. As a result, the radiation that harmed her body also got into her notebooks. Even today, Marie's notebooks are too radioactive to handle safely.

After the Curies discovered radium, many companies wanted to use it in their products. Marie and Pierre could have made money by patenting their process for collecting radium. Instead, they believed radium belonged to everyone. They felt other scientists should be allowed to find ways for radium to benefit the world.

Marie is the only person ever awarded two Nobel Science Prizes in different subjects. She won the Nobel Prize in Physics in 1903. Her 1911 Nobel Prize was in chemistry.

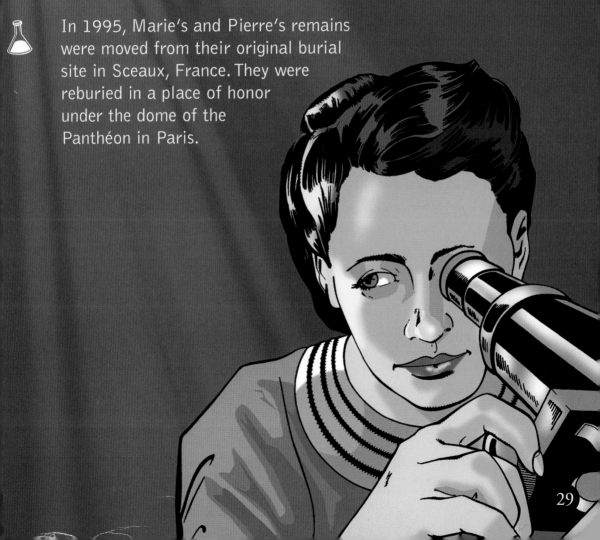

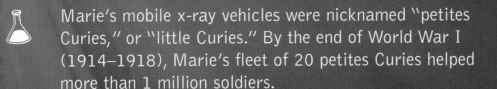 Marie's mobile x-ray vehicles were nicknamed "petites Curies," or "little Curies." By the end of World War I (1914–1918), Marie's fleet of 20 petites Curies helped more than 1 million soldiers.

Marie and Pierre studied ways radioactivity could be used in medicine to help people. But the discovery of radioactivity also had a negative side. It led to the creation of the atomic bombs the United States dropped on Japan near the end of World War II (1939–1945).

In 1995, Marie's and Pierre's remains were moved from their original burial site in Sceaux, France. They were reburied in a place of honor under the dome of the Panthéon in Paris.

GLOSSARY

element (EL-uh-muhnt)—a basic substance in chemistry that cannot be split into simpler substances

persecute (PUR-suh-kyoot)—to cause to suffer

physics (FIZ-iks)—the study of matter and energy, including light, heat, electricity, and motion

radiation (ray-dee-AY-shuhn)—tiny particles sent out from radioactive material

radioactivity (ray-dee-oh-ak-TIV-uh-tee)—a process in which atoms break apart and create a lot of energy

uranium (yu-RAY-nee-uhm)—a silver-white radioactive metal that is the main source of nuclear energy

INTERNET SITES

FactHound offers a safe, fun way to find Internet sites related to this book. All of the sites on FactHound have been researched by our staff.

Here's how:
1. Visit *www.facthound.com*
2. Choose your grade level.
3. Type in this book ID **0736864865** for age-appropriate sites. You may also browse subjects by clicking on letters, or by clicking on pictures and words.
4. Click on the **Fetch It** button.

FactHound will fetch the best sites for you!

READ MORE

Gogerly, Liz. *Marie Curie.* Scientists Who Made History. Austin: Raintree Steck-Vaughn, 2001.

Lassieur, Allison. *Marie Curie: A Scientific Pioneer.* Great Life Stories. New York: Franklin Watts, 2003.

Orr, Tamra. *Marie Curie.* The World Was Never the Same. Minneapolis: Lake Street Publishers, 2003.

Pettigrew, Mark. *Radiation.* Science World. North Mankato, Minn.: Stargazer Books, 2004.

Waxman, Laura Hamilton. *Marie Curie.* History Makers Bios. Minneapolis: Lerner, 2004.

BIBLIOGRAPHY

Curie, Eve. *Madame Curie: A Biography.* Garden City, N.Y.: Doubleday, Doran and Company, Inc., 1938.

Dry, Sarah. *Curie.* London: Haus Publishing, 2003.

Goldsmith, Barbara. *Obsessive Genius: The Inner World of Marie Curie.* New York: W. W. Norton, 2005.

Pflaum, Rosalynd. *Grand Obsession: Madame Curie and Her World.* New York: Doubleday, 1989.

INDEX